Council of the
INSPECTORS GENERAL
on INTEGRITY and EFFICIENCY

Quality Standards

for

Inspection and Evaluation

January 2012

Council of the Inspectors General
on Integrity and Efficiency

Authority
Section 11 of the Inspector General Act of 1978 (5 U.S.C. app. 3.), as amended (IG Act).

Mission
The mission of the Council of the Inspectors General on Integrity and Efficiency (CIGIE) shall be to address integrity, economy, and effectiveness issues that transcend individual Government agencies; and increase the professionalism and effectiveness of personnel by developing policies, standards, and approaches to aid in the establishment of a well trained and highly skilled workforce in the Offices of Inspectors General (OIG).

CIGIE Inspection and Evaluation Committee
Provides leadership for the CIGIE Inspection and Evaluation community's effort to improve agency program effectiveness by maintaining professional standards; leading the development of protocols for reviewing management issues that cut across departments and agencies; promoting the use of advanced program evaluation techniques; and fostering awareness of evaluation and inspection practice in OIGs. The Committee provides input to the CIGIE Professional Development Committee on the training and the development needs of the CIGIE Inspection and Evaluation community.

Message from the Chairman of the
CIGIE Inspection and Evaluation Committee

Since it was first issued in 1993, the "Quality Standards for Inspections" has provided a solid framework for inspections and evaluation work by Federal Offices of Inspector General (OIG). Over the years, these standards have been broadly embraced by OIGs and have thus been instrumental in building our strong reputation for impartiality, reliability, and credibility.

The Inspector General Reform Act of 2008 (IG Reform Act) provided that members of the Council of the Inspectors General on Integrity and Efficiency (CIGIE) "shall adhere to professional standards developed by the Council" (§ 11(c)(2) of the IG Reform Act). In June 2010, CIGIE officially adopted the "Quality Standards for Inspections" as the professional standards for all inspection and evaluation work performed by member organizations. The IG Reform Act requires compliance with these standards.

For this 2011 edition of the "Quality Standards for Inspection and Evaluation," the Inspection and Evaluation (I&E) Committee has made technical changes that bring the document into full compliance with the IG Reform Act, including replacing all references to the "PCIE" (President's Council on Integrity and Efficiency) and the "ECIE" (Executive Council on Integrity and Efficiency) with CIGIE. However, except for these technical changes and mandating adherence to the "Quality Standards" when conducting I&E work, the standards as revised in 2005 are largely unchanged.

I want to personally thank everyone who worked to revise these standards and to give special recognition to the I&E Roundtable for its leading role on this project. The value and relevance of our work depends on just this sort of cooperative effort.

Daniel R. Levinson
Chairman, Inspection and Evaluation Committee

TABLE OF CONTENTS

Page

STANDARDS

APPENDIXES

Within the Inspector General community, inspections and evaluations have long afforded OIGs a flexible and effective mechanism for oversight and review of Department/Agency programs by using a multidisciplinary staff and multiple methods for gathering and analyzing data. These *Quality Standards for Inspection and Evaluation* have been developed as a framework for performing both inspection and evaluation work.

Inspections and evaluations are systematic and independent assessments of the design, implementation, and/or results of an Agency's operations, programs, or policies. They provide information that is timely, credible, and useful for agency managers, policymakers, and others. Inspections or evaluations can be used to determine efficiency, effectiveness, impact, and/or sustainability of agency operations, programs, or polices. They often recommend improvements and identify where administrative action is necessary. Other uses of inspections and evaluations include but are not limited to:

- providing factual and analytical information;
- measuring performance;
- determining compliance with applicable law, regulation, and/or policy
- identifying savings and funds put to better use;
- sharing best practices or promising approaches;
- assessing allegations of fraud, waste, abuse, and mismanagement.

The inspection and evaluation function at each Department/Agency is tailored to its unique mission. Some OIGs make a distinction between inspection and evaluation work. Thus, to be responsive to the needs of the Inspector General community, it is important that the standards for conducting inspections and evaluations not be overly prescriptive, or the very flexibility and timeliness that make inspections and evaluations such valuable tools would be lost. It is the responsibility of each OIG that conducts inspections or evaluations to develop internal written policies and procedures to ensure that all such work complies with these *Quality Standards for Inspection and Evaluation* as well as the Inspector General Act of 1978, as amended, and any other legislation, regulation, or standards applicable to an organization's operations.

The Council of the Inspectors General on Integrity and Efficiency endorse the *Quality Standards for Inspection and Evaluation* and, in compliance with the Inspector General Reform Act of 2008, expects the consistent application of these standards throughout the Inspector General community. The standards are reviewed periodically to ensure their continuing relevancy and sufficiency.

QUALITY STANDARDS FOR INSPECTION AND EVALUATION

Inspections and Evaluations organizations should strive to conduct their operations in the most efficient and effective manner possible, which serves to enhance the credibility of the organizations. The following standards are established by the Council of the Inspectors General on Integrity and Efficiency (CIGIE) to guide all inspection work performed by Offices of Inspector General (OIG). The term "inspection" includes evaluations, inquiries, and similar types of reviews that do not constitute an audit or a criminal investigation. The term "inspector" is used generically to refer to the individual conducting such work.

COMPETENCY

The standard for inspection work is:

The staff assigned to perform inspection work should collectively possess adequate professional competency for the tasks required.

The inspection organization needs to ensure that the personnel conducting an inspection collectively have the knowledge, skills, abilities, and experience necessary for the assignment, which should include:

- Knowledge of evaluation methodologies; familiarity with the concepts, processes, and assumptions of the program or activity being inspected; the capacity to conduct a broad interdisciplinary inquiry; knowledge of qualitative and quantitative analysis; writing and oral briefing skills; information technology related capabilities; and knowledge of Inspector General statutory requirements and directives.

- The ability to develop a working familiarity with the organizations, programs, activities, and/or functions identified for inspection. When reviewing technical or scientific topics, it may be appropriate to use the services of a subject matter expert. Expertise may be determined by the individual having a related degree, license, certification, experience, etc.

- Managerial skills for supervisors, team leaders, and lead inspectors.

The Inspector General community has developed a guide regarding core competencies for inspection organizations and inspectors, as well as a guide for general skill levels for inspectors, which are included as appendixes to this document. Inspection organizations should have a process for recruitment, hiring, continuous development, and evaluation of staff to assist the organization in maintaining a workforce that has adequate competence. The nature, extent, and formality of the process will depend on various factors, such as the size of the inspection organization, its work, and its structure. These factors will also affect the staffing needs of an organization. For example, an inspection organization may need to employ personnel or hire specialists who are knowledgeable, skilled, or experienced in such areas as accounting, statistics, law, engineering, information technology, public administration, economics, or social sciences.

OIGs should strive to provide inspectors with 80 hours of training biennially, but should minimally provide 40 hours of training biennially. Appropriate training may include evaluation/ inspection training, such as program analysis; writing; technical training; and career development training, such as in managerial skills.

OIGs should have internal policies and procedures for issuance and utilization of credentials.

INDEPENDENCE

The standard for inspection work is:

> *In all matters relating to inspection work, the inspection organization and each individual inspector should be free both in fact and appearance from personal, external, and organizational impairments to independence.*

Inspectors and inspection organizations have a responsibility to maintain independence so that opinions, conclusions, judgments, and recommendations will be impartial and will be viewed as impartial by knowledgeable third parties. The independence standard should be applied to anyone in the organization who may directly influence the outcome of an inspection and includes both Government and private persons performing inspection work for an OIG.

Inspection organizations and inspectors should be alert to possible impairments to independence and should avoid situations that could lead reasonable third parties with knowledge of the relevant facts and circumstances to conclude that the inspection organization or inspectors are not independent and, thus, are not capable of exercising objective and impartial judgment in conducting and reporting on an inspection. Impairments to independence, either in fact or appearance, need to be resolved in a timely manner. The actions of OIG staff should adhere to the "Standards for Ethical Conduct for Employees of the Executive Branch" and Federal conflict-of-interest laws. Inspection organizations should have internal policies and procedures for reporting and resolving real or perceived impairments to independence.

Inspection organizations that provide other professional services should consider whether providing these services creates an independence impairment either in fact or appearance that adversely affects their independence for conducting inspections. Inspection organizations should not (1) provide noninspection services that involve performing management functions or making management decisions or (2) inspect their own work or provide noninspection services in situations where the noninspection services are significant/material to the subject matter of inspections. Inspection organizations that provide other professional services should refer to the "Government Auditing Standards" issued by the United States Government Accountability Office, which, although specific to auditing, provides detailed guidance relevant to handling the provision of such services.

Inspection organizations and inspectors need to consider three general types of impairments to independence—personal, external, and organizational. If one or more of these impairments affect an inspection organization's or an inspector's capability to perform work and report results impartially, that organization or inspector should either decline to perform the work or, if the situation necessitates that the work cannot be declined, the impairment(s) should be reported in the scope section of the inspection report.

1. Personal Impairments

   Personal impairments of staff members result from relationships and beliefs that might cause inspectors to limit the extent of an inquiry, limit disclosure, or weaken or slant inspection findings in any way. Inspectors are responsible for notifying the appropriate officials within

3

their respective inspection organizations if they have any personal impairment to independence. It is impossible to identify every situation that could result in a personal impairment, but the following are examples of personal impairments:

- having an immediate or close family member who is a director or officer of the entity being inspected or is in a position with the entity to exert direct and significant influence over the entity or the program being inspected. Immediate or close family members include spouses, domestic partners, dependents (whether or not related), parents, siblings, and nondependent children;

- having direct or significant/material indirect financial interest in the entity or program being inspected;

- having responsibility for managing an entity or for decisionmaking that could affect operations of the entity or program being inspected; for example, as a director, officer, or other senior member of the entity, activity, or program being inspected or as a member of management in any decisionmaking, supervisory, or ongoing monitoring function for the entity, activity, or program under inspection;

- having involvement with the preparation, maintenance, or authorization of official records/ documents associated with the entity, activity, or program under inspection;

- having preconceived ideas toward individuals, groups, organizations, or objectives of a particular program that could bias the inspection;

- having biases, including those induced by political, ideological, or social convictions, that result from employment in or loyalty to a particular type of policy, group, organization, or level of government; or

- seeking employment with an inspected organization during the conduct of the inspection.

2. External Impairments

Factors external to the OIG may restrict work or interfere with an inspector's ability to form independent and objective opinions and conclusions. External impairments to independence occur when inspectors are deterred from acting objectively and exercising professional skepticism by pressures, actual or perceived, from management or employees of the inspected entity or oversight organizations. For example, if any of the following conditions exist, the OIG would not have complete freedom to make an independent and objective judgment, which could adversely affect the work:

- external interference or influence that could improperly or imprudently limit or modify the scope of an inspection or threaten to do so, including pressure to reduce inappropriately the extent of work performed in order to reduce costs or fees;

- external interference with the selection or application of inspection procedures or in the selection of transactions to be examined;

- unreasonable restrictions on the time allowed to complete an inspection or issue a report;

- external interference in the assignment, appointment, or promotion of inspection personnel;

- restrictions on funds or other resources provided to the inspection organization that adversely affect the inspection organization's ability to carry out its responsibilities;

- authority to inappropriately overrule or influence an inspector's judgment as to the appropriate content of the report;

- threat of replacement over a disagreement with the contents of an inspection report, an inspector's conclusions, or the application of criteria; and

- influences that jeopardize an inspector's continued employment for reasons other than incompetence, misconduct, or the need for inspection services.

When external factors restrict an inspection or interfere with an inspector's ability to form objective opinions and conclusions and the inspector cannot remove the limitation, the inspector should report the limitation in accordance with the respective OIG's internal policies and procedures.

3. Organizational Impairments

Inspection organizations need to be free from organizational impairments to independence. An organization's ability to perform work and report the results impartially can be affected by its place within a Department/Agency and the structure of the Department/ Agency. Inspection organizations within OIGs established by the Inspector General Act of 1978, as amended, derive organizational independence from the statutory safeguards to independence established by the Act.

However, if an inspector believes there is an organizational impairment that could affect his or her inspection work, he or she should report the matter in accordance with the respective OIG's internal policies and procedures.

PROFESSIONAL JUDGMENT

The standard for inspection work is:

Due professional judgment should be used in planning and performing inspections and in reporting the results.

This standard requires inspectors to exercise reasonable care and diligence and to observe the principles of serving the public interest and maintaining the highest degree of integrity, objectivity, and independence in applying professional judgment to all aspects of their work. Due professional judgment requires that:

- OIGs follow professional, Department/Agency, and organizational standards and that inspection work be in accordance with all applicable laws, rules, and regulations.

- Inspections are conducted in a timely, diligent, and complete manner, using appropriate methods and techniques.

- Evidence is gathered and reported in a fair, unbiased, and independent manner and report findings, conclusions, and recommendations are valid and supported by adequate documentation.

- At all times, the actions of OIG staff conform to high standards of conduct, including adherence with the "Standards for Ethical Conduct for Employees of the Executive Branch" and Federal conflict-of-interest laws.

- OIG staff coordinates inspection results with appropriate officials.

Inspectors should use professional judgment in selecting the type of work to be performed and the standards that apply to the work, defining the scope of work, selecting the inspection methodology, determining the type and amount of evidence to be gathered, and choosing the tests and procedures for their work. Professional judgment also should be applied when actually performing the tests and procedures and when evaluating and reporting the results of the work.

In conducting an inspection, inspectors may employ the methods of inquiry most appropriate for the object of study. They may rely on the work of others after satisfying themselves regarding the quality of the work by appropriate means. Such work may include work performed by other OIG units, the Government Accountability Office, Department/Agency internal studies, Department/Agency contracted studies, or studies by private research and academic organizations.

Professional judgment requires inspectors to exercise professional skepticism, e.g., questioning and critically assessing evidence, throughout the inspection. Inspectors should use the knowledge, skills, and experience called for by their profession to diligently gather evidence and objectively evaluate its sufficiency, competency, and relevancy. Inspectors should seek persuasive evidence and should not presume honesty or dishonesty on the part of those who are providing evidence.

The exercise of professional judgment allows inspectors to obtain reasonable assurance that material misstatements or significant inaccuracies in data will likely be detected if they exist. However, absolute assurance is not attainable because of the nature of evidence and the characteristics of fraud. Therefore, while this standard places responsibility on each inspector and inspection organization to exercise professional judgment in planning and performing an assignment, it does not imply unlimited responsibility or infallibility on the part of either the individual inspector or the inspection organization.

QUALITY CONTROL

The standard for inspection work is:

Each OIG organization that conducts inspections should have appropriate internal quality controls for that work.

Each OIG organization that conducts inspections should develop and implement written policies and procedures for internal controls over its inspection processes/work to provide reasonable assurance of conformance with organizational policies and procedures, the "Quality Standards for Inspection and Evaluation," and other applicable policies and procedures. The nature and extent of these internal controls and their associated documentation will be dependent on a number of factors, such as the size and structure of the organization and cost-benefit considerations. As appropriate, organizations should seek to have quality control mechanisms that provide an independent assessment of inspection processes/work. Documentation of the execution of quality control mechanisms should be retained for a sufficient period of time to allow for evaluation and use in conjunction with other quality control mechanisms.

A key aspect of inspection quality control is adequate supervision. Supervision provides important judgment and an additional level of oversight to the work done by subordinate, often less experienced, staff. Supervisors should work with inspection team members to reach agreement as to the work the team will do and how they are to proceed. The team also should have a clear understanding of the purpose of the inspection and what it is expected to accomplish. Supervisory reviews help ensure that:

- the inspection is adequately planned;

- the inspection work plan is followed, unless deviation is justified and authorized;

- the inspection objectives are met; and

- the inspection findings, conclusions, and recommendations are adequately supported by the evidence.

PLANNING

The standard for inspection work is:

Inspections are to be adequately planned.

The standard for inspection planning is intended to ensure that appropriate care is given to selecting inspection topics and preparing to conduct each inspection, to include coordinating inspection work and avoiding duplication. The selection of an inspection topic should consider the relevancy of the topic and the significance/impact of potential outcomes, and these points should be of continuing consideration throughout the inspection. Department/Agency and other customers' needs also should be a consideration in selecting inspection topics.

The planning standard is also intended to ensure that inspection topics are appropriately researched and that the objective(s) of the inspection are clearly understood. Research, work planning, and coordination should be thorough enough, within the time constraints of the inspection, to ensure that the inspection objectives are met. In pursuing this standard, the following should be appropriately addressed:

- **Coordination**
  Inspection planning includes coordinating planned activities with other inspection, audit, and investigative entities, as well as appropriate organizations that could be affected by the activities. Internal and external constraints should be considered when planning inspection activities. Inspectors should be flexible in their plans, within reasonable limits. Any internal reviews performed by the entity to be inspected or by outside professional organizations should be considered and reviewed to determine applicability to the inspection. In addition, when an inspection addresses a topic that is cross-cutting or affects other governmental organizations, the OIG may consider conducting a joint or coordinated review with those other organizations' OIGs.

- **Research**
  Consistent with the inspection objectives, inspection research includes a review of existing data, discussions

with program and other appropriate officials, literature research, and a review of pertinent Web sites and other Internet-accessible materials to gather information that will facilitate understanding of the program or activity to be inspected. Research should help to identify the criteria applicable to the evaluation of the program or activity. Examples of possible criteria include: laws, regulations, policies, procedures, technically developed standards or norms, expert opinions, prior periods' performance, performance of similar entities, performance in the private sector, and best practices of leading organizations. Research should attempt to identify the results of previous reviews that may be relevant to the inspection, and inspectors should follow up on known significant findings and recommendations that directly relate to the current inspection. Inspectors need to assess the validity and reliability of the data gathered.

- **Work plan**
  An inspection work plan should be developed that clearly defines the inspection objective(s), scope, and methodology. It may also include inspection time frames and work assignments. Adequate planning also entails ensuring that sufficient staff with the appropriate collective knowledge, skills, abilities, and experience is assigned to the inspection effort. As work on an inspection progresses, the work plan may need revision to address new information.

During inspection planning, consideration should also be given to whether the inspection is likely to involve sensitive or classified information. If this is so, appropriate steps must be taken to ensure the proper protection of that information. The sensitivity or classification of information needs to be a consideration throughout the inspection process.

DATA COLLECTION AND ANALYSIS

The standard for inspection work is:

The collection of information and data will be focused on the organization, program, activity, or function being inspected, consistent with the inspection objectives, and will be sufficient to provide a reasonable basis for reaching conclusions.

With regard to collecting data, the following guidance should be addressed whenever appropriate:

- The sources of information should be described in the supporting documentation in sufficient detail so that the adequacy of the information, as a basis for reaching conclusions, can be assessed.

- Information should be of such scope and selected in such ways as to address pertinent questions about the objectives of the inspection and be responsive to the informational needs and interests of specified audiences.

- The procedures and mechanisms used to gather information should ensure that the information is sufficiently reliable and valid for use in meeting the inspection objectives. For example, inspectors need to ensure the validity and reliability of data obtained from computer-based systems if they are significant to the inspectors' findings. Inspectors will use professional judgment in determining whether information is sufficiently reliable and valid.

- Confidentiality, as appropriate, should be afforded to sources of information consistent with the Inspector General Act of 1978, as amended; the internal policies of each OIG; and other applicable laws and statutes. The Inspector General Act of 1978, as amended, states that the Inspector General shall not, without the consent of the employee or unless the Inspector General determines that such a disclosure is unavoidable, disclose the identity of a Department/Agency employee providing a complaint or information concerning the possible violation of law, rules, or regulations; mismanagement; waste of funds; abuse of authority; or a substantial and specific danger to public health or safety. OIGs should develop and

11

implement procedures for maintaining the confidentiality of individuals providing information. Inspectors must carefully monitor their actions and words to not inappropriately reveal the source of information.

- Appropriate safeguards should be provided for sensitive information, such as personal and proprietary data, as well as classified information. Inspectors General should ensure they have appropriate procedures for handling such information.

In analyzing data, the following guidance should be considered:

- Data should be reviewed for accuracy and reliability; and, if necessary, the techniques used to collect, process, and report the data should be reviewed and revised to ensure the accuracy and reliability of inspection results.

- Qualitative and quantitative information gathered in an inspection should be appropriately and logically presented and documented in work papers, to ensure supportable interpretations.

- Inspection procedures should provide for supervisory review and other safeguards to protect the inspection findings and reports against distortion by the personal feelings and biases of any party to the inspection.

- Findings often have been regarded as containing the elements of criteria; condition; effect; and, when problems are found, cause. However, the elements needed for a finding depend entirely on the objectives of the inspection. Thus, a finding or set of findings is complete to the extent that the inspection objectives are satisfied and the report clearly relates those objectives to the applicable elements of a finding.

EVIDENCE

The standard for inspection work is:

Evidence supporting inspection findings, conclusions, and recommendations should be sufficient, competent, and relevant and should lead a reasonable person to sustain the findings, conclusions, and recommendations.

Evidence may take many forms, including physical, testimonial, documentary, and analytical. Physical evidence is obtained by an inspector's direct review or observation of people, property, or events and should be appropriately documented. Testimonial evidence is obtained through inquiries, interviews, or questionnaires. Documentary evidence consists of created information, such as letters, contracts, grants, memorandums, and files. Analytical evidence includes computations, benchmarking, trending, comparisons, and rational arguments.

The following guidelines should be considered regarding evidence:

- Evidence should be sufficient to support the inspection findings. In determining the sufficiency of evidence, inspectors should ensure that enough evidence exists to persuade a knowledgeable person of the validity of the findings.

- To be competent, evidence should be reliable and the best obtainable by using reasonable collection and evaluation methods. The following presumptions are useful in judging the competency of evidence:

  o evidence obtained from an independent source may be more reliable than that secured from an organization being inspected;

  o evidence developed under an effective system of internal controls generally is more reliable than that obtained where such controls are lacking or unsatisfactory;

  o evidence obtained through direct physical examination, observation, or computation may be more reliable than evidence obtained through less direct means;

  o original documents generally are more reliable than copies; and

  o testimonial evidence obtained from an individual who is not biased or who has complete knowledge about the area usually is more competent than testimonial evidence obtained from an individual who is biased or has only partial knowledge about the area.

- Relevance refers to the relationship of evidence to its use. The information used to prove or disprove an issue must have a logical relationship with, and importance to, the issue being addressed.

RECORDS MAINTENANCE

The standard for inspection work is:

All relevant documentation generated, obtained, and used in supporting inspection findings, conclusions, and recommendations should be retained for an appropriate period of time.

Supporting documentation is the material generated and collected as part of an inspection that, when effectively organized, provides an efficient tool for data analysis and a sound basis for findings, conclusions, and recommendations that address the inspection objectives. Supporting documentation should also provide:

- a record of the nature and scope of inspection work performed, and

- information to supervisors and team leaders enabling them to properly manage inspections and evaluate the performance of their staff. Supervisory and team leader review should be evidenced in the inspection documentation.

Inspection organizations should establish policies and procedures for the safe custody and retention of inspection documentation. Inspection documentation should be retained and disposed of in accordance with applicable legal and administrative requirements and schedules, e.g., those established by the National Archives and Records Administration and the respective Department/Agency. Documentation generated by the Department/Agency and used to support inspection findings, such as lengthy reports, could be retained by the Department/Agency so long as the OIG fully references these documents and is confident that the documentation in question could not be lost, destroyed, or altered.

TIMELINESS

The standard for inspection work is:

Inspections should strive to deliver significant information to appropriate management officials and other customers in a timely manner.

To be of maximum use, inspections need to be conducted and reporting needs to be completed in a timely manner. This helps to ensure the work is current and relevant. During an inspection, it may be appropriate to provide interim reporting of significant matters to appropriate officials. Such reporting is not a substitute for a final report, but it does serve to alert the appropriate officials to matters needing immediate attention, so corrective action may be initiated. The following guidance should be considered regarding timeliness:

- Time frames should be flexible in response to changing priorities.

- Time frames established during planning are subject to change due to unforeseen circumstances, such as the need to expand the scope of an inspection or the need to add additional objectives.

FRAUD, OTHER ILLEGAL ACTS, AND ABUSE

The standard for inspection work is:

In conducting inspection work, inspectors should be alert to possible fraud, other illegal acts, and abuse and should appropriately follow up on any indicators of such activity and promptly present associated information to their supervisors for review and possible referral to the appropriate investigative office.

During an inspection, inspectors should be alert to any indicators of fraud, other illegal acts, or abuse (behavior that is deficient or improper when compared with behavior that a prudent person would consider reasonable and necessary business practice given the facts and circumstances). While the identification of such activities is not usually an objective of an inspection, it is necessary to have a clear understanding of the action required if such circumstances are discovered.

Inspectors should be aware of vulnerabilities to fraud and abuse associated with the area under review in order to be able to identify possible or actual illegal acts or abuse that may have occurred. In some circumstances, conditions such as the following might indicate a heightened risk of fraud:

- the absence of internal controls;

- inadequate "separation of duties," especially those that relate to controlling and safeguarding resources;

- transactions that are out of the ordinary and are not satisfactorily explained or documented, such as unexplained adjustments in inventories or other resources;

- missing or altered documents or unexplained delays in providing information;

- false or misleading information; or

- a history of impropriety, such as past reviews with findings of questionable or criminal activity.

In pursuing indications of possible illegal acts or abuse, inspectors should exercise professional judgment so as to ensure they do not interfere with potential investigations and/or legal proceedings. If possible illegal behavior arises, inspectors should promptly present such information to their supervisors for review and possible referral to the appropriate investigative office.

REPORTING

The standard for inspection work is:

Inspection reporting shall present factual data accurately, fairly, and objectively and present findings, conclusions, and recommendations in a persuasive manner.

Various means may be used to report on the results of inspection work, e.g., written reports, oral presentations, videos, or slide presentations. Regardless of the means used, there should be retrievable documentation of the reporting. The content of the reporting will be affected by the specific means used and the purpose it is serving. Reporting should be timely, complete, accurate, objective, convincing, clear, and concise.

16

Inspection reporting normally should describe the objective(s), scope, and methodology of the inspection and state that the inspection was conducted in accordance with the "Quality Standards for Inspection and Evaluation." Also, inspection reporting should provide the reader with the context in which the subject matter being inspected should be viewed, such as the impact or significance of the program/activity being reviewed, to help ensure the focus is not too narrowly drawn and to give clearer understanding of the impact of any report recommendations. Reporting language should be clear and concise and, while recognizing that some inspections deal with highly technical material, should be written in terms intelligible to the intended recipients and informed professionals.

Inspection reporting frequently is structured in terms of findings, conclusions, and recommendations. Findings should be supported by sufficient, competent, and relevant evidence. Conclusions should be logical inferences about the inspected program or activity based on the inspection findings. Typically, each finding requiring corrective action should be addressed by one or more recommendations directed to the management official(s) who have the authority to act on them. Recommendations normally should not be prescriptive in nature; rather, they should be crafted in a manner that lays out what needs to be corrected or achieved. When appropriate, inspectors should solicit advance review and comments from responsible officials regarding the content of the report and should include the comments or a summary thereof in the report.

Care must be taken to ensure that, as applicable, the confidentiality of individuals providing information is appropriately maintained in the inspection reporting process.

Written inspection reports should be distributed to the appropriate officials responsible for taking action on the findings and recommendations. Further distribution will be subject to the internal policies of each OIG and fully comply with all requirements contained in the Privacy Act; the Freedom of Information Act; and security and other applicable laws, regulations, and policies.

FOLLOWUP

The standard for inspection work is:

Appropriate followup will be performed to ensure that any inspection recommendations made to Department/Agency officials are adequately considered and appropriately addressed.

Ultimate inspection success depends on whether necessary corrective actions are actually completed. Therefore, each OIG should take steps, as necessary, to determine whether officials take timely, complete, and reasonable actions to correct problems identified in inspection reports and agreed on by management. Specific followup actions shall be guided by the followup and resolution policies of each OIG, in accordance with Office of Management and Budget Circular No. A-50, as amended.

Followup helps ensure actions are undertaken and completed within a reasonable time. Management notification that an action has been completed within the agreed-on time constitutes reasonable assurance and can be the basis for "closing" an action for followup purposes. However, the OIG should perform, as appropriate, followup work to verify whether agreed-on corrective actions were fully and properly implemented. When planning followup activities, OIGs should assess whether the work would be most effectively accomplished utilizing the staff that conducted the original work or other staff members. Also, in planning and conducting new inspections, prior recommendations that relate to the new inspection should be considered and followed up on to the extent practicable.

PERFORMANCE MEASUREMENT

The standard for inspection work is:

Mechanisms should be in place to measure the effectiveness of inspection work.

Consistent with the intent of the Government Performance and Results Act of 1993, it is important to be able to demonstrate the positive results that inspections contribute to the more effective management and operation of Federal programs. The nature and extent of performance measurement will be affected by a number of factors, such as the size and structure of the organization performing inspections. For example, measures may be established that capture inspection results and recommendations collectively with those of other OIG components. Performance measurement for inspections should focus on the outputs (i.e., number of implemented recommendations), and the resultant outcomes (i.e., changes in policy). Optimum performance measurement captures the impact of an inspection and may include such things as monetary savings, enforcement of laws, or legislative change.

WORKING RELATIONSHIPS AND COMMUNICATION

The standard for inspection work is:

Each inspection organization should seek to facilitate positive working relationships and effective communication with those entities being inspected and other interested parties.

The OIG and the Department/Agency should strive to:

- Foster open communication at all levels. With limited exceptions, primarily related to investigative-type work, the OIG should keep the Department/Agency advised of its work and its findings on a timely basis and strive to provide information helpful to the Department/Agency at the earliest possible stage. Surprises are to be avoided.

- Interact with professionalism and respect. OIGs should act in good faith.

- Recognize and respect the mission and priorities of the Department/Agency. Each OIG should work to carry out its functions with a minimum of disruption to the primary work of the Department/Agency.

- Be thorough, objective, and fair. The OIG must perform its work thoroughly, objectively, and with consideration to the Department's/Agency's point of view and should recognize Department/Agency successes in addressing challenges or issues.

- Be engaged. While maintaining OIG statutory independence of operations and recognizing that OIGs need to conduct work that is self-initiated, congressionally requested, or mandated by law, OIGs should interact with Department/Agency management to identify any specific needs or priorities management may have regarding the reviews to be conducted by the OIG.

- Be knowledgeable. The OIG will continually strive to keep abreast of Department/Agency programs and operations, and Department/Agency management should be kept appropriately informed of OIG activities and concerns being raised in the course of OIG work.

- Provide feedback. OIGs should implement mechanisms, both formal and informal, to ensure prompt and regular feedback.

During an inspection, inspectors should appropriately communicate information about the process and the nature of the inspection to the various parties involved to help them understand such things as the inspection objective(s), time frames, data needs, and reporting process. Inspectors should use their professional judgment and comply with their respective organizations' policies and procedures to determine the form, content, and frequency of communication. Communication should be appropriately documented in the associated inspection records.

GUIDE FOR CORE COMPETENCIES FOR INSPECTION ORGANIZATIONS AND INSPECTORS

This guide was developed by the Inspector General community to identify the core competencies that each inspection organization should strive to have as an organization, as well as the competencies that are desirable for a journeyman inspector and senior management.

Organizational Competencies

- Leadership

    ✓ Vision
    ✓ Continual Learning
    ✓ Results Orientation
    ✓ Integrity

- Team Skills

    ✓ Team Problem Solving
    ✓ Time Management

- Management

    ✓ Accountability
    ✓ Customer Service
    ✓ Strategic Thinking

- Occupational Mastery

    ✓ Department/Agency and Mission Knowledge
    ✓ Oral Communication
    ✓ Written Communication

Journeyman Level Competencies

- Leadership

    ✓ Results Orientation
    ✓ Integrity

- Team Skills

    ✓ Team Problem Solving
    ✓ Time Management

- Management

  - ✓ Project Management
  - ✓ Strategic Thinking

- Occupational Mastery

  - ✓ Department/Agency and Mission Knowledge
  - ✓ Evaluation Methods and Techniques
  - ✓ Oral Communication
  - ✓ Written Communication

Senior Management Competencies

- Leadership

  - ✓ Vision
  - ✓ Political Skills
  - ✓ Influencing/Negotiation with External Groups
  - ✓ Results Orientation
  - ✓ Leading People
  - ✓ Integrity

- Team Skills

  - ✓ Team Problem Solving
  - ✓ Time Management

- Management

  - ✓ Accountability
  - ✓ Decisiveness
  - ✓ Strategic Thinking

- Occupational Mastery

  - ✓ Department/Agency and Mission Knowledge
  - ✓ Oral Communication

GUIDE FOR GENERAL SKILL LEVELS
FOR INSPECTORS*

Skills	GS Grade						
	5	7	9	11	12	13	14
1. OIG statutes, regulations, policies, & procedures	X	X	X	X	X	X	X
2. Ethics code of conduct	X	X	X	X	X	X	X
3. Basic research	X	X	X	X	X	X	X
4. Computer applications	X	X	X	X	X	X	X
5. Data collection techniques	X	X	X	X	X	X	X
6. Data analysis	X	X	X	X	X	X	X
7. Use of computers	X	X	X	X	X	X	X
8. Disclosure & Privacy Act	X	X	X	X	X	X	X
9. Fraudulent, abusive, & illegal acts	X	X	X	X	X	X	X
10. Documenting evidence	X	X	X	X	X	X	X
11. Interviewing		X	X	X	X	X	X
12. Basic report writing			X	X	X	X	X
13. Administrative process			X	X	X	X	X
14. Inspection work plans			X	X	X	X	X
15. Designing survey instruments				X	X	X	X
16. Statistical sampling				X	X	X	X
17. Site selection and approving records for field work				X	X	X	X
18. Advanced report writing				X	X	X	X
19. Packaging inspection reports				X	X	X	X
20. Training inspection team members					X	X	X
21. Briefings					X	X	X
22. Marketing inspection products					X	X	X
23. Legislative process					X	X	X
24. Departmental budget process					X	X	X
25. Managing & coordinating inspection team activity						X	X
26. Preparing congressional testimony						X	X
27. Dealing with the media, public, & industry						X	X

*This appendix is intended as a guide only. It is recognized that, among other things, grade structure and position descriptions for staff vary between OIGs, which can affect the applicability of this guidance.

www.ingramcontent.com/pod-product-compliance
Lightning Source LLC
Chambersburg PA
CBHW070941290526
45795CB00003B/1104